Gerty and Gus

Become Friends

Kim Langham, PhD.

ISBN: 9781660306985

DEDICATION

This book is dedicated to my two boys.
They are my everything!
I am reminded every day I look at them
just how blessed I am.
Thank you, Lord, for two beautiful and amazing gifts!

ACKNOWLEDGMENTS

I want to thank my Illustrator, Barbara Scheer, for her amazing talents and skills and for her time spent painting the images within this book. She has been so wonderful to work with, and I appreciate all her support.

I also wish to thank my Creator for blessing me with so many gifts!

He is my biggest fan!

ABOUT THE AUTHOR

Currently residing in the South, Kim was born in Missouri. She earned her degrees in sports medicine, elementary education and curriculum and instruction and taught K-12 for about twelve years. She is passionate about education and enjoys teaching others. Being in the classroom, and observing the interactions among learners, she was inspired to write books that would help children improve their relationship and interaction experiences. She presently teaches online and creates courses for higher education.

ABOUT THE ILLUSTRATOR

Born and raised in the Midwest, Barbara Scheer is a self-taught artist who has enjoyed drawing and painting all her life. She has painted many custom wall murals in doctor offices and private residences. Barbara lives in Missouri and is the mastermind and creator of a local, annual festival that promotes art and creativity.

"A great day for a journey!
I wonder what I'll find.
High to low and head to toe,
Surely things of all kind!"

"Hello!
Every morning, when I wake, I take off on a journey with the hope
of learning something new! Today, Gus is going to join me!
Come along with us on our adventure."

"I'm so excited that you're joining me on my adventure today, Gus. My friend, Lulu the ladybug, is also going along," said Gerty.
"I am very excited, too, Gerty. I cannot wait to see what we will find!"
It is so nice to meet you, Lulu" said Gus.
"It is a pleasure to meet you, too," said Lulu.

As Gerty, Gus and Lulu started off on their journey, Gus stopped in his tracks. "Gerty?" asked Gus. "What's a friend?"

Gerty stops, turns around and responds. "A friend is someone who is supportive, respectful and polite. It is someone you trust. You might share similarities, get along well and enjoy spending time together."

"Wow! That is a lot!" Gus replied, as he started walking again. A few seconds later, Gus stops. "Gerty? What does supportive mean?" asked Gus.

Gerty turns to answer Gus. "Supportive means to be loyal, helpful and encouraging," answered Gerty. "Lulu is supportive because she is always there for me," she continued.

"I bet she helps you with all sorts of things, too!" exclaimed Gus.
As they all continued walking, Lulu smiled and said, "Gerty and I
get along really well. We go everywhere together."

But Gus was still trying to understand what it meant to be friends, so he continued to ask questions. "Gerty? What do respectful and polite mean?" he questioned.

Gerty was happy to answer his questions, though. Being so social, she loves to talk, so she replied, "To respect means to admire, to think highly of and to treat with care. Polite means to be nice."

"Lulu respects me, and I respect her because we care about and are very nice to each other," she added.

Gus was enjoying learning more about what it meant to be friends, but he had one more question to ask. "What does trust have to do with being friends?"

"Trust is having confidence in another person. You can rely on him or her. Lulu is trustworthy because I can always count on her to do what she says she will do," responded Ger y.

"I do what I say I will do, so I can be trusted, Gerty, and I am very strong, so I can support you," said Gus.
Gerty and Lulu giggled at Gus's response.

"I bet Lulu also flies around with you and supports you as you swing from branch to branch," said Gus.

"She sure does, Gus! She also helps to keep other bugs off my bananas while I eat them!" Gerty exclaimed. All three of them giggled at Gerty's comment as they nibbled on bananas together.

"You and Lulu seem to have a lot in common and get along well," Gus stated. "I cannot fly, but I like to crawl around and relax in the water. I am also usually very quiet and shy, while you are very social and outgoing. Do you think we can be friends, Gerty?" asked Gus.

"Of course, we can, Gus! Just because we have some differences does not mean we cannot be friends. You and I share several similarities, too! I also enjoy playing in the water," responded Gerty. "I bet we have more in common, Gus!" she added.

"Really, Gerty? What else do we have in common?" asked Gus.

"Well, we both can live in many parts of the world, we enjoy hanging out by trees and grassy areas," Gerty answered. "And, we both like the same kinds of food, too!" she exclaimed as she bit into another banana.

"You're an omnivore?" Gus asked in disbelief.

"Yes! We are both omnivores!" replied Gerty.

"I did not know that, Gerty! I wonder what else we have in common," Gus said excitedly.

"Lulu and I like to play ball, Gus.," stated Gerty. "Do you like to play ball?" she asked.

"I sure do!" exclaimed Gus with excitement.

"See? There's another thing we have in common, Gus!" replied Gerty.

"I guess it is true that you don't have to have everything alike to be friends with someone. Thanks, Gerty!" Gus responded.

Friends have a lot in common
and many similarities, true.
But they may have some differences
and be opposites, too.
The real thing to remember
about being a friend,
Is to be respectful and caring
and supportive to the end.

Gerty looked high to low and head to toe.

"Hey, Gus! Guess what?" exclaimed Gerty. "I think we just found something on our adventure!"

"What did we find, Gerty?" Gus asked with anticipation.

Gerty blurted it out in excitement! "We each just found a friend! You are my new friend, and I am your new friend, Gus."

"Wow! You are right, Gerty!" exclaimed Gus. "This is so neat!"